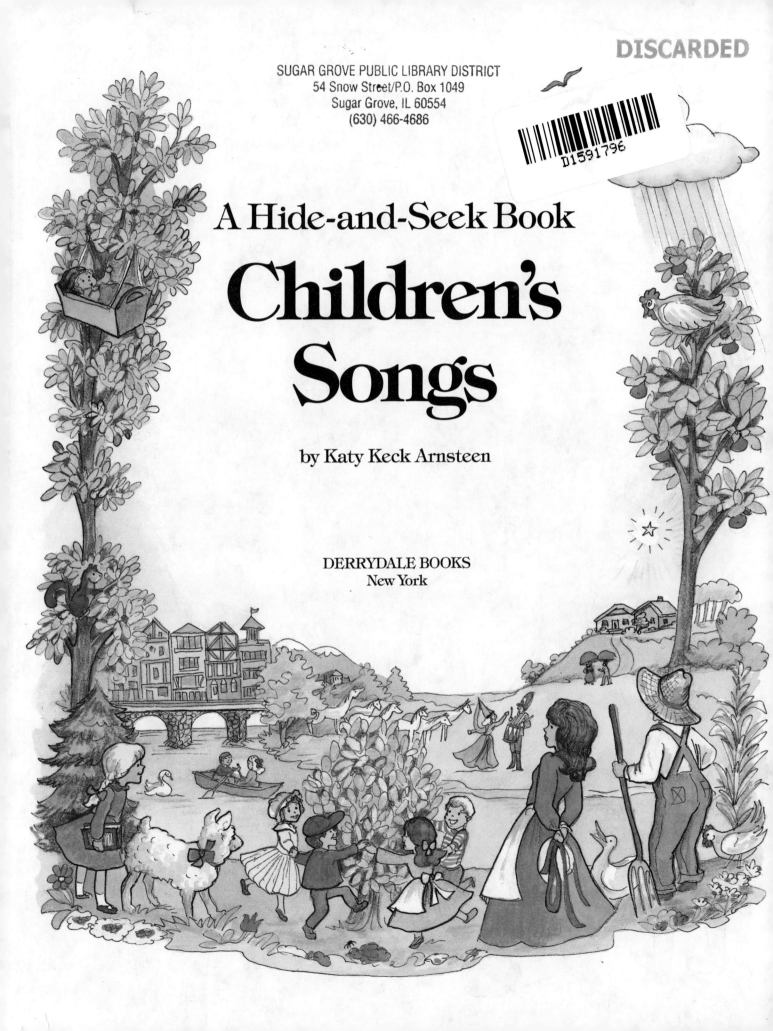

A Hide-and-Seek Book

Children's Songs

by Katy Keck Arnsteen

DERRYDALE BOOKS
New York

Mary Had a Little Lamb

Mary lost her lamb on the playground. Can you find it?

It's Raining, It's Pouring

The old man who's snoring left his slippers out in the rain.
Can you find them?

This Old Man, He Played One

The dog is waiting for someone to throw him a bone. Can you find it?

The Itsy Bitsy Spider

The itsy bitsy spider washed down the water spout. Can you find it?

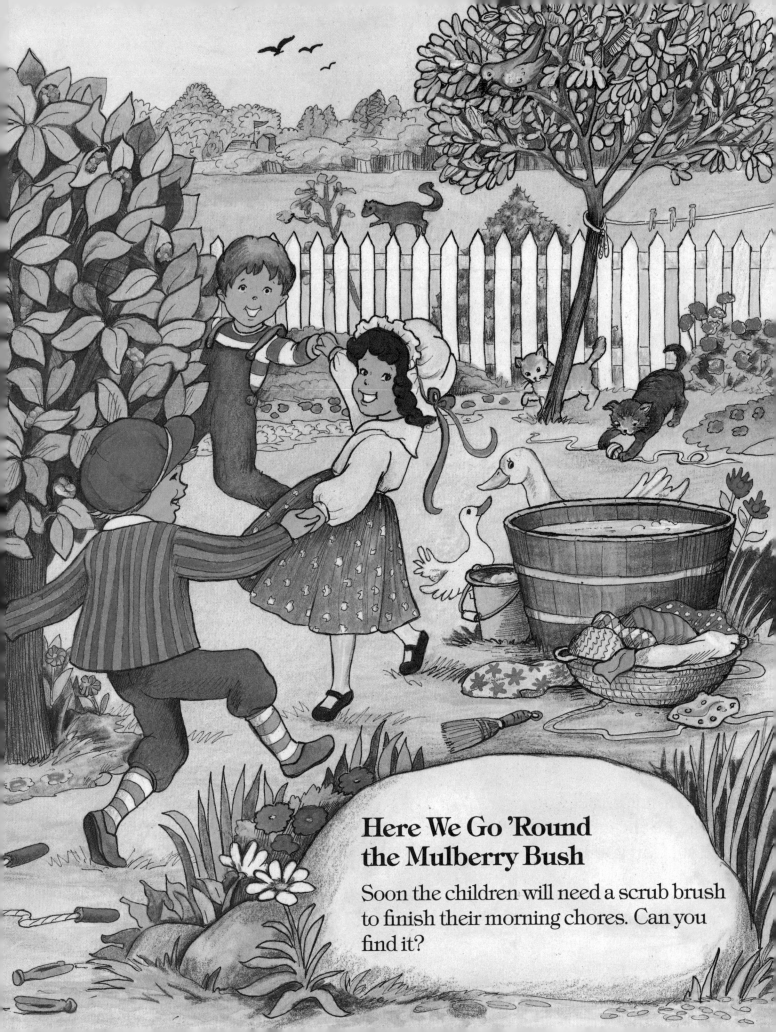

Here We Go 'Round the Mulberry Bush

Soon the children will need a scrub brush to finish their morning chores. Can you find it?

Old MacDonald Had a Farm

Old MacDonald can't find his duck, but he can hear it quacking. Can you find it?

Row, Row, Row Your Boat

The boy lost one of his oars while he was rowing. Can you find it?

Rock-a-bye Baby

The rocking baby has lost one bootie.
Can you find it?

Twinkle, Twinkle Little Star

Four stars are not high in the sky like the other star. Can you find them?